GW00382873

Images of Plymouth :
Stonehouse

Images of Plymouth:
Stonehouse
by
Derek Tait

Driftwood Coast Publishing

Frontispiece : The Parish Church of St Peter the Apostle,
Wyndham Square after enemy bombing in the 1940s.

First published 2011

Driftwood Coast Publishing
Derek Tait, Plymouth, PL5 1JU.
© Derek Tait, 2011

The right of Derek Tait to be identified as the Author
of this work has been asserted in accordance with the
Copyrights, Designs and Patents Act 1988.

All rights reserved. No part of this book may be reprinted
or reproduced or utilised in any form or by any electronic,
mechanical or other means, now known or hereafter invented,
including photocopying and recording, or in any storage or retrieval
system, without the permission in writing from the publishers.

Contents

Acknowledgements

Photo credits: The Derek Tait Picture Collection and Steve Johnson (Cyberheritage).
I have tried to track down the copyright holders of all photos used and apologise to anyone who hasn't been mentioned.

Bibliography

Books:
Images of England : Plymouth by Derek Tait (Tempus 2003).
Plymouth at War (Tempus 2006).
A topographical dictionary of England by Samuel Lewis (1835).
Plymouth and Plymothians by Andrew Cluer and Ron Winram (Aberdeen University Press 1985).
Plymouth and Plymothians - More Photographs and Memories by Andrew Cluer (Lantern Books 1975).

Websites:
Brian Moseley's Plymouth Data website at: www.plymouthdata.info
Steve Johnson's Cyberheritage site at: www.cyber-heritage.co.uk

Newspapers
Evening Herald
Western Morning News

Driftwood Coast Publishing
© Derek Tait 2011

Introduction

The history of the area now known as Stonehouse dates back very a long way. There is evidence of prehistoric activity and it is thought that Romans also once occupied the area. It is believed that a stone house may have stood on the area near to Stonehouse Creek in Roman times. However, if this was the case, there are no remains of it.

At Newport Street, near Stonehouse Bridge, an ancient burial place was found in 1882. Although everything has now been destroyed, reports at the time suggested that it may have been a Roman crematorium.

Stonehouse was called Hepeston or Hippeston in ancient times. In the 13th century, the land was owned by Robert the Bastard who was the illegitimate son of King Henry I.

During the reign of Henry III, it had just one house which was the seat of Joel de Stonehouse.

The land later passed to the Durnford family and then to the Edgcumbes through marriage when Joan Durnford married Sir Piers Edgcumbe in 1493. In 1515, Sir Piers fortified the town wall near to his manor house in Stonehouse and constructed tidal corn mills across Stonehouse Creek in 1525.

Stonehouse was for a while known as East Stonehouse to distinguish it from the village of West Stonehouse which once stood near Cremyll at Mount Edgcumbe.

Emma Place in Stonehouse was named after Lady Emma Edgcumbe who was born in 1791 and Caroline Place was named after her sister. Emma died in 1878.

Notable buildings include the Royal William Victualling Yard, the Royal Naval Hospital (now Millfields) and the Royal Marine Barracks.

The Second World War devastated the area. Much of Chapel Street and Stonehouse Bridge were destroyed.

Today, parts of Stonehouse have been rejuvenated. The Royal William Victualling Yard and the Royal Naval Hospital are now private apartments and dwellings and much of Durnford Street has been tidied up. Some parts of Stonehouse have seen better days but there is continued building work which constantly changes the face of the area.

This book not only takes in the history of Stonehouse but also the nearby areas which had an affect on the town. I hope that it will increase people's knowledge of Stonehouse and also prove to be interesting and enjoyable.

One

Prehistory

There are several limestone caverns within the Plymouth area where the remains of prehistoric life have been found. An article from the Evening Herald for the 9th November, 1960 carried a report about prehistoric caverns at Stonehouse and read:

'Stonehouse's prehistoric limestone caverns, discovered in the 18th century and since lost to modern knowledge have, it is believed, been rediscovered by builders excavating foundations for a new warehouse in George Street. Directing a pneumatic drill into limestone boulders, a workman found the rock giving way to expose a 10ft shaft with two long fissures squeezing from it. Remains of prehistoric rhinoceroses, horses, oxen, deer and other animals were once found in the caverns but were destroyed when the Athenaeum was blitzed in the last war.'

I haven't been able to find any follow up to this article but it's amazing that all this probably still exists beneath the streets of Stonehouse and it's such a shame that the remains found in the 1700s were destroyed in the war.
The story of Cattedown Man is well known and his remains were discovered in limestone caves in the Cattedown area of the city in 1887. With him were the bones of 15 early humans together with the remains of woolly rhinoceros, woolly mammoth, deer and lion dating from the ice age. The remains are approximately 140,000 years old and are the oldest remains discovered in the British Isles.
Prehistoric remains have been found in Ernesettle Woods, at Mutley and Keyham as well as Stonehouse.
It's incredible to think what lies beneath our feet but also incredible that very little of this history ever seems to be mentioned. I certainly haven't read anything at all about the Stonehouse Caverns in the last 40 years. The location of the Cattedown caverns is meant to be a secret, for fear of fossil hunters etc, but it's well known that they are located beneath the fuel depot there. It would be incredible to be able to visit them and it seems a shame that the area is off limits to local residents.

Two

The Romans

Although it has always been supposed that the Romans didn't travel further down into the Westcountry than Exeter, there is evidence to suggest that there was a presence in the area now known as Plymouth. The name Stonehouse dates back to Saxon times and is thought to have come from an old stone house, a building now long gone, which once stood in the area. If this was the case, only the Romans would have had the capabilities of constructing such a building.

In 1882, a Roman crematorium was discovered at Newport Street just below Stonehouse Bridge. It contained small tombs, about four feet by two feet, containing human bones and ashes. Unfortunately, it has all long since been destroyed.

There are many other accounts of a Roman presence within Plymouth. Roman Way leading downwards from Kings Tamerton is said to be the route that the Romans took on their way to Cornwall. A Roman signalling station is thought to have existed at the top of the hill. Roman Way was previously called, 'Old Wall's Lane', in the 1800s, which would suggest an earlier settlement. The area was excavated in 1934 by a Mr E N Masson Phillips who discovered an early fortification. Soapwort has been found growing nearby and this was a herb used by the Romans and is usually only found on the site of an old settlement.

Roman Way lies on the second oldest route traceable in Plymouth which travels east to west from Saltash to Plympton. There seems to be no record of Roman coins being found at Roman Way although a hoard of Roman coins was found at Compton Giffard in 1894 and this lies on the same route. There were a thousand coins and none were later than AD 280. It was suggested by the British Museum that the coins could have been used to pay the Romans that were stationed in the area. A similar hoard was found at Marazion near Penzance.

Roman coins have also been found at Whitleigh and by the Plym.

The Romans left Britain in 410AD.

In the early 1980s, the Evening Herald reported the find of a Roman coin on the shores of the River Plym. The article read:

'Eighteen hundred years ago this coin must have been lost on the shores of the River Plym. It has been identified as a bronze 'as' and depicts on one side Antoninus Pius, who was Emperor of Rome from 138 to 161 AD, and on the other, Annona, the godess of the corn-harvest.

This valuable clue to Plymouth's past was found recently, in the mud of the River Plym near Marsh Mills by Peter Jones, 15, of Efford who was digging not for Romans but for worms.'

Stonehouse Bridge today near to where a Roman crematorium was discovered in 1882.

Three

Around Stonehouse

'A topographical dictionary of England' by Samuel Lewis published in 1835 described Stonehouse at the time as:

STONEHOUSE, EAST (St. George), a parish, in the suburbs of the borough of Plymouth, Roborough Division of the county of Devon, containing 9571 inhabitants. This place, originally called Hipperston, was, in the reign of Henry III, the property of Joel de Stonehouse, from whom it derives its present name; it was then situated more southerly, but, after subsequent improvements and extension to the northward, the ancient buildings were allowed to fall into decay. It includes several good streets, which are mostly paved, and lighted with gas. The houses are of neat and respectable character and the inhabitants are well supplied with water by means of pipes leading from the reservoir of the Devonport Water Company, situated in the parish of Stoke Damerel, and from a fine stream brought into the town under an act passed in the reign of Elizabeth. A very handsome quadrangle of Greek architecture, enclosing the new chapel of St. Paul, is now in progress in the south-western part of the town. A communication was made with Devonport by means of a stone bridge across Stonehouse Creek, erected at the joint expense of the Earl of Mount Edgcumbe and Sir John St. Aubyn. The tolls are let annually, at a public survey, and the income derived from them is very considerable. Higher up the creek, to the north, a bridge has been recently erected, affording a passage to Stoke. On the Devil's Point (which commands, perhaps, the finest prospect of Mount Edgcumbe) is the picturesque ruin of a blockhouse, erected in the time of Elizabeth; and over this old edifice is a modern battery, occupied by the Royal Marine Artillery. At a short distance is Eastern King's battery, commanding the mouth of the Hamoaze. There is also a fort for the protection of the creek. The three towns of Stonehouse, Plymouth and Devonport are brilliantly lighted from the gas-works in this parish. The gasometer presents a conspicuous object from the road from Plymouth to Devonport. The road to the ferry at New Passage passes through this place. In Stonehouse Pool are convenient quays for merchant vessels and, in addition to the general business arising from the maritime relations of this town, and its naval and military establishments, there are some large manufactories for varnish used in the dockyards, soap, and tallow. A customary market is held on Wednesday, in a neat and convenient building in Edgcumbe Street and there are fairs on the first Wednesday in May, and the second Wednesday in September. By the act to amend the representation, recently passed, the township of Stonehouse has been included within the limits of the newly enfranchised borough of Devonport. The town is within the jurisdiction of the county magistrates, who hold their sessions in the town hall at Devonport. A manorial court leet and baron is held annually.

Among the most important public establishments is the Royal Naval Hospital, for the reception of wounded seamen and marines, opened in 1762. It is situated on an eminence near the creek and comprises of ten buildings, each containing six wards, each ward affording accommodation for about twenty patients, with a chapel, store-room, operating-room, small-pox ward, and dispensary. They form an extensive quadrangle, ornamented on three sides with a piazza and the entire edifice, with its spacious lawn, is said to occupy an area of 24 acres. In 1795, the government of this institution was vested in a post-captain. The other officers are, the first and second lieutenants, physician, surgeon, dispenser, chaplain, agent, and steward. The chapel is open to the public. The Royal Marine barracks, on the west shore of Millbay, comprise a handsome range of buildings forming an oblong square, and are adapted for the accommodation of about 1000 men. The Long Room barracks, built chiefly of wood, will contain 900. A new victualling establishment has been lately erected at Devil's Point, upon a scale of great magnitude. It is approached through a granite gateway and double colonnade of singular beauty, and the various ranges of building are surprisingly magnificent. Among the more remarkable features of the work are, the removal of 300,000 cubic yards of limestone rock, and the erection of a granite sea-wall, 1500 feet in length, the foundation of which was laid by means of a diving bell. The water for the brewery is supplied, at the rate of 350 tons per day, from the Plymouth Leat. It first runs into a reservoir capable of receiving 2000 tons and is thence conveyed through iron pipes into a second basin of 6000 tons. The Royal Military Hospital is situated on the opposite side of the creek, in the parish of Stoke-Damerel, its government is similar to that of the Naval Hospital.

Stonehouse was formerly a chapelry in the parish of St. Andrew, Plymouth. The living is a perpetual curacy, in the archdeaconry of Totnes, and diocese of Exeter with a net income of £197. The patron, the Vicar of St. Andrew's, Plymouth, and the impropriators, Corporation of Plymouth.'

Stonehouse Town Hall was erected between 1849 and 1850. It was Italian in style. It was designed by Fuller and Gingell of Bristol. The stone for the building was given by the third Earl of Mount Edgcumbe and stood at the junction of Emma Place and Stonehouse Street. A police station adjoined the building. The Town Hall was the centre of local government in Stonehouse until 1914 when the three towns were amalgamated. The amalgamation was partly due to the Admiralty who, in the event of war, wanted to deal with one authority rather than the three towns of Plymouth, Devonport and Stonehouse. Part of the building included an ante-natal and baby clinic, a library and also entertained ballroom dancing and recitals. Unfortunately, it was destroyed by enemy bombing in the Second World War.

Emma Place.

A close-up view of some of the houses that once stood in the street.

Emma Place.

The Stonehouse Town Hall can be seen at the far end of the street. Emma Place has changed completely over the years and many of the older buildings have disappeared although some still remain.

King George V's proclamation on 11th May, 1910 which is shown taking place by Stonehouse Town Hall.

Four

Stonehouse Bridge

Before the Stonehouse Bridge was built, the only way to cross the river was by ferry or by taking the road around Millbridge. Lord Mount Edgcumbe, who was the Lord of the Manor of Stonehouse, was authorised by an Act of Parliament to construct a bridge linking Devonport and Stonehouse in 1767. He was joined in the venture by Sir John St Aubyn who was Lord of the Manor of Stoke Damerel.

The bridge was opened in 1773 and the toll for pedestrians was a halfpenny which led to the bridge being called Halfpenny Bridge. A cart drawn by one horse was charged 2d return and this increased to 3d for two horses and 6d for wagons with more than two horses.

The approach to the bridge was via Stonehouse Lane, which later became King Street, and High Lane. Union Street wasn't built until 1815. The General Tolls Company Ltd bought the rights to the fares taken on the bridge in 1890 for £122,000, which would have been an incredible amount at the time. The Earl of Mount Edgcumbe and Lord St Levan both had shares in the company.

An act of parliament in 1923 allowed Plymouth Town Council to purchase the toll rights for a sum of £100,000.

It was destroyed by enemy bombing during the Second World War but was later rebuilt.

In 1972, the creek was partly filled in with 600,000 tons of rubble which allowed 19 acres of recreational land to be created.

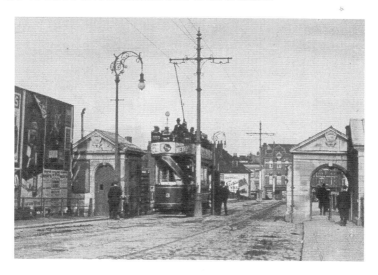

An early view of the bridge. The hoarding on the right reads, 'Give her Bovril.'

Stonehouse Bridge with Plymouth Breweries in the background.

The view of the bridge, on the previous page, shows Plymouth Breweries Limited in Chapel Street in the background. The Prince Albert Public House can be seen in the middle of the picture. There were once many pubs in Chapel Street. The 1861 census mentions the Freemasons Arms, the Globe and Laurel, the Military Arms, the Prince George, the Prince Regent and the Red Lion as well as the Prince Albert. Chapel Street once ran from the Eastern end of the Stonehouse Bridge towards Edgcumbe Street joining the junction at Emma Place. During the Second World War, Chapel Street was badly damaged and much of St George's Church, which gave its name to Chapel Street, was also destroyed.

Above the bridge is a sign which reads, 'Memorial, Wreaths and Pessells.'

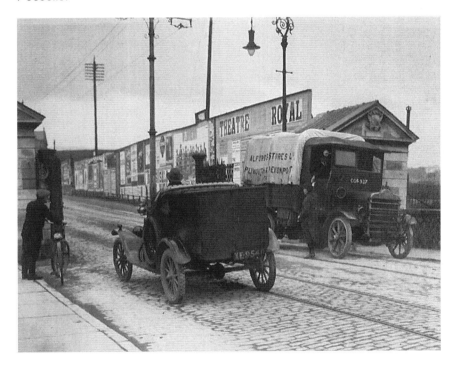

Early motor transport.

The tram lines still remain (trams ran in Plymouth until 1945) although there are many less horse-drawn wagons and early motor vehicles now can be seen passing over the bridge. To the right, is an advert for the Theatre Royal. The writing on the lorry reads, 'Alfords Stores Ltd - Plymouth and Devonport.'

17

The driver of a horse and cart stops to talk to a woman as he crosses the bridge. Coming in the other direction is another horse and carriage as well as a woman with a handcart perhaps with goods to sell in Plymouth. The poster hoardings advertising local businesses and events stretch right across the bridge. Devonport can be seen in the background.

This photo shows a later shot of the bridge looking much the same as it does today. The brewery building can be seen with adverts for 'Prize Bitter' and 'Double Brown Ale'.

Houdini in chains.

P A L A C E,   P L Y M O U T H.
TWICE NIGHTLY, 7 AND 9.
MONDAY, AUGUST 16TH, 1909, AND DURING THE WEEK.
Performances commence 10 minutes earlier on Saturday only.
H O U D I N I,
The Original Handcuff King and Jail Breaker.
BILLY YOUNG   JACKLEY TRIO.
MAY MAIDMENT.   STEWART and MORGAN.
TWO MOE BOYS.   THE PALASCOPE.
B I L L Y   W I L L I A M S
The Man in the Velvet Suit

An advert for Houdini's show at the Palace Theatre, Union Street.

A hundred years ago, Plymouth and Stonehouse, of course, were totally different places. There was no television and no talking films so when a world famous artist such as Houdini performed at the Palace Theatre of Varieties during August 1909, the event drew a huge crowd. Combined with his stage show, Houdini also leaped off Halfpenny Bridge in chains in front of the many spectators who had gathered to see him. Of course, he manage to escape to loud applause from the gathered crowd. Houdini appeared in front of packed audiences at the Palace Theatre between the 16th and 23rd August, 1909. Between 1900 and 1914, Houdini played at over a hundred venues within the UK. Houdini was a very generous man, When he performed his show in Edinburgh, he noticed how many children were without shoes. He performed a special show just for the Scottish youngsters and made sure that there were three hundred pairs of shoes so none would go away barefooted. There wasn't nearly enough shoes for the children that turned up so Houdini took them all to the nearest cobbler and made sure that everyone was given a pair.

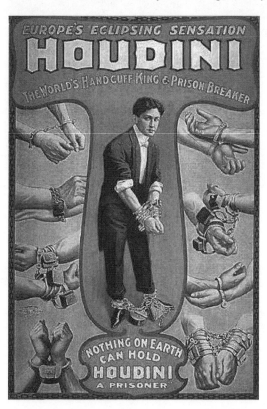

The following piece is taken from a local newspaper of the day and captures the excitement of Houdini's act:

HOUDINI AT PLYMOUTH.
AN INEXPLICABLE TRICK.

Harry Houdini, expert prison breaker and handcuff manipulator, who has been mystifying the Plymouth public at the Palace Theatre of Varieties this week, gave a marvellous exhibition of his wonderful powers last evening. The test arose from a challenge issued by five mechanics and joiners of the Devonport Dockyard that they could make a box from which Houdini could not escape. The 'handcuff king' accepted the challenge, which was decided at the second house at the Palace yesterday. The challenge excited great interest and every seat was booked and the building packed to overflowing. Many hundreds were unable to gain admission. The mechanics filed onto the stage with the box, which was of inch thick wood, and fastened together with 2½ inch wire nails. As it has been exhibited at the Palace for some days, the challengers, to preclude any suggestion of it having been tampered with, went around every edge and inserted handfuls of fresh nails. Houdini, who was received with tremendous applause, soon stepped into the box, and was, after it was seen by the audience that he was really inside, securely nailed in. Previously, ventilation holes were drilled in two of the sides. A strong rope was then passed around the box with half hitches, and was itself then nailed to the wood. The performer was then heard to ask if everything was all right, and, on being assured that that was the case, the curtain was placed around the box. The latter had also been thoroughly examined by the Dockyardmen and a committee of the audience, who were on the stage. Houdini was also searched, but no tools were found on him. During the interval of waiting, the orchestra played several well known songs, which the audience sang to pass away the time. After twelve minutes, the band suddenly stopped and the 'house' was in uproar. Houdini had appeared, perspiring profusely, while during his confinement he had also discarded his dress coat. Cheer upon cheer greeted the performer and everyone, the challengers, committee and audience, admitted themselves to be thoroughly at a loss how to explain the trick. The box was in exactly the same condition as when Houdini was nailed in. There was no sign of an opening anywhere. The nails, rope and cover were also as securely fastened as they were previously. The box, during the test, was at the request of the challengers, placed on a carpet and not on the stage flooring. The Dockyardmen accepted their defeat and each heartily congratulated Houdini on his success. The box was subsequently inspected by the audience.

At the first house, a gentleman offered Houdini £10 if he could escape from a strait jacket after being fastened in it by a number of sailors. The challenge was accepted but Houdini got free in a little over seven minutes. The ten pounds will today be handed over to the Mayor with the suggestion that £5 shall be sent to the Variety Artistes' Benevolent Fund and £5 to a local charity.

THE DIVE FROM STONEHOUSE BRIDGE.

Rain did not deter an immense crowd from assembling at Stonehouse Bridge last evening to witness Houdini, 'the handcuff king', doubly manacled, dive from that structure. Punctually at six o'clock, the intrepid American appeared on the bridge, nude accept for a pair of white knickers. He seemed anxious to make the plunge but for a few seconds, he was prevented by the presence of boats below. Mr. Field, the manager of the Palace and Houdini's men, who were also in boats, shouted to the occupants of the obstructing craft and they tardily cleared the course.

Houdini was speedily shackled by his chief assistant. An arm-iron was placed around the upper part of his arms and fastened at his back, after which his hands were secured with handcuffs. Without betraying the slightest sign of trepidation, fettered and hampered as he was by 18lbs. weight of iron and his hands bound behind his back, he stood for a few seconds in an upright posture, drew several deep inhalations until his lungs were visibly distended and then hurled his body forward into space. In falling, he gave a backward kick in order to balance his body. His head cleaved the placid waters and Houdini disappeared from view.

Then followed a period of suspense and to alter slightly Macaulay's 'Horatius' :-

'The spectators in dumb surprise,
With parting lips and straining eyes.
Stood gazing where he sank.'

Houdini's head reappeared above the surface in the space of forty-five seconds amid the plaudits of the multitude. He had succeeded in releasing himself from his fetters and at once swam ashore, jumped into the cab in which he had driven out and assumed his clothes on the way back to the New Palace Theatre.

Five
Transport

Transport played a major part in linking Stonehouse, Devonport and Plymouth. When Union Street was built in 1815, it enabled traffic to flow freely between the three towns.

The Plymouth, Stonehouse and Devonport Tramways Company constructed the first tramway in 1872. The trams were emerald green and cream and were pulled by two horses. Additional horses were added at Stonehouse Bridge to take the tramcars up the steep hill towards Devonport.

The route started at Derry's Clock and passed through Stonehouse and crossed the Stonehouse Bridge and terminated in Cumberland Road, Devonport. On the first day of the tram service on 12th February 1872, free rides were given to passengers, with the regular service starting the next day. The service's route was extended from Chapel Street to Fore Street in 1875.

A horse drawn tram on Stonehouse Bridge in the late 1800s. Extra horses have been added to the tramcars to make the journey uphill easier. A man is riding one of the horses and a spare horse can be seen on the right of the picture.

A car with white-walled tyres stops to pay the toll on the bridge. A huge hoarding for the Theatre Royal can be seen in the background.

Tram number 4 at the Stonehouse end of Union Street, c.1910.This tram belonged to the Plymouth, Stonehouse and Devonport Tramways, a company that ran between 1901 and 1922. At the time, they had a fleet of 16 electric trams. This, the number 4, was brightly decorated with adverts including one for the Western Morning News.

A tram at Stonehouse, c.1930's. Part of the Plymouth Corporation
Tramways, this tram's destination would have been 'Theatre' via Union
Street from Devonport, one of the most used lines in Plymouth. On its
side are its destinations including North Road and Fore Street. This one
features an advert for Jacob's Crackers.

Millbay Station

The station was opened in 1849 and was known at the time as Plymouth Millbay. The station was expanded in 1859. Stonehouse can be seen in the background.

The Duke of Cornwall Hotel with Millbay Station on the left.

The hotel was built to serve passengers from the nearby station and opened in 1862.

Six
Union Street

Union Street was constructed in 1815. It had previously been called New Road and the area had formerly consisted of marshland called Sourepool. John Foulston designed the street, incorporating a distinct feature, the Octagon. The street united the three towns of Plymouth, Devonport and Stonehouse. It ran from Derry's Clock to the junction of Manor and Phoenix Street. It then became Union Street, East Stonehouse, and stretched to the junction at Brownlow Street. It then joined Edgcumbe Street until it met the Stonehouse Bridge.
In incorporated Union Terrace, Lockyer Terrace, The Octagon, Squire Terrace, Devonshire Terrace, Flora Place and Sussex Place.

Two elderly men stop for a chat in this photo taken in the early 1900s. Behind them is 'The New Penny Bazaar' where everything appears to be one penny. Perhaps this was the fore runner to today's 'pound shop'! Originally, Marks and Spencers started their business as the Penny Bazaar.
The shop next door's sign advertises, 'Cricket, Football and Tennis Shoes.'
On the right in the background, can be seen the Union Street arch.

In 1872, Plymouth's first tramway along Union Street was opened. It was controlled by the Plymouth, Stonehouse and Devonport Tramway Company and formed part of a direct link between the three towns.

To make way for the New Palace Theatre of Varieties in the late 1890s, several buildings in Union Street were knocked down. These included premises belonging to Frederick Charles Burner, the tobacconist; Mark Durbin, a provision dealer; Jonathan Crowl, the butcher and John Shepheard, a bootmaker.

There used to be a turnpike at the Phoenix and Manor Street junction and also a toll booth on the Stonehouse Bridge. However, this ended in 1843 when the Stonehouse Turnpike Trust was dissolved.

For a while, Union Street was the home of the wealthy and a guidebook from 1823 stated:

'The buildings are neat and handsome, and the streets straight and commodious, particularly those of Durnford Street, Emma Place, Edgcumbe Street and Union Street. These are almost entirely occupied by genteel families, chiefly those of naval and military officers, and other persons holding situations under government. The addition of Union Street is an improvement of the greatest importance, it affords a spacious thoroughfare, and presents a succession of neat and uniform buildings.'

An early view looking down Union Street. Burton's can be seen on the right beside Williams and H Samuel.

In 1849, a cholera epidemic broke out in Union Street and this was believed to have been caused by works at the nearby Millbay Station which led to blocked drains and caused the overflow of sewerage to nearby homes.

A busy scene in Union Street in the 1890s. There seems to be a procession of horses and carts and many people have turned out to watch. The horse at the front of the picture has many ribbons and has a sign saying '4th'. The tramlines can be seen clearly on the road although it appears that the trams have been halted for the event.

The area became the haunt of servicemen and during the 1930s, there were 30 public houses in Union Street.

There's certainly a lot going on in this shot. Establishments that can clearly be seen include The Posada, H Samuel, Burton's and Williams. The Posada advertises 'American Cocktails' on the side of its building. Near to the Posada is a Union Jack flag on a pole and the street is full of people. The clock on the left appears to read twenty to six so I wonder if this is a summer scene showing people returning home after work? Two cars can be seen on the right and a tram is heading towards the photographer.

The Union Street arch took rail traffic away from Millbay Station, which stood opposite the Duke of Cornwall Hotel, where the Pavilions stands today.

H & G Simonds the Brewers situated off the Octagon.

The Birkhead Hotel at 48 Union Street.

A busy scene in Union Street showing many pedestrians and a couple of trams. On the left can be seen 'Olivers' and on the right, 'The Posada'.

The Grand Theatre is on the left and the hoarding advertises the play, *'The Girl Who Lost her Character'* which toured England in the early 1900s. A tram can be seen further along the road and in the distance is Plymouth's main shopping area.

A photo showing the Grand Theatre in 1880. The horse-drawn tram is packed with passengers. An advert for 'The Metropole' appears on the front. The Palace Theatre of Varieties can just be seen in the background so the tram must be heading along Union Street towards Stonehouse Bridge.

Servicemen walking by The Farley Hotel in Union Street. The street has always been very popular with Naval personnel.

Colonel Cody, 'Buffalo Bill'.

When Buffalo Bill visited Plymouth on the 3rd June 1904, he brought with him a troop of Red Indians who toured with his Wild West Show. For the first time, Red Indians could be seen sitting on street corners in the Stonehouse and Union Street areas of the city. It must have been an amazing sight when people's only experience of Red Indians was through stories read about cowboys and Indians in newspapers, comics or seen in early silent movies. Children would have been particularly fascinated by them as their only knowledge of Indians would be from tales told about Geronimo or Custer's Last Stand.

Sitting Bull.

The one thing that was noted at the time about the visiting Red Indians was that they couldn't handle their drink and notices appeared in drinking houses which read, 'No Indians to be served'. Nowadays, this might seem to appear as being racist but at the time, the problem was actually caused by them getting drunk too quickly and being overly rowdy.

Willie Sitting Bull was one of the Indians who accompanied Buffalo Bill to Britain. He was the only son of Sitting Bull (pictured). Sitting Bull himself had originally taken part in the show when it toured America. It's amazing to think how things had changed in America, especially for the Indians, in just two generations of a family. Willie regularly took part in mock battles which featured the defeat of Custer at Little Big Horn.

The show at the Exhibition Fields, Pennycomequick must have been an amazing sight. It's interesting that there are still people living in Plymouth today that remember their relatives telling them of the Wild West show and a time when Red Indians filled the streets of the town.

The above photo shows a busy Union Street with many pedestrians. A lone tram can be seen in the middle of the picture. It's certainly changed a great deal over the years and many of the buildings seen here have long since disappeared.

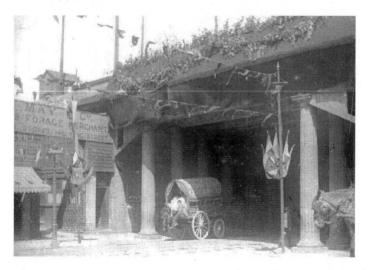

Union Street arch.

The building on the left of the photo houses May & Co. Their sign advertises themselves as 'Forage Merchants' and gives their business address as 146 King Street. Underneath the bridge is a covered wagon with children sat on the back. The street is decorated with bunting and other decorations so there must have been some sort of celebration going on.

Seven
The Palace Theatre

The theatre in Union Street was originally called the New Palace Theatre of Varieties and was opened on the 5th September, 1898. The opening show featured Adele and May Lilian who were billed as the Levey Sisters. They performed Persian and hunting songs and were followed by an acrobatic act called The Six Craggs. Other acts that night included Walter and Edie Cassons who performed a vaudeville act, a comedian called Harry Comlin and a roller skater called Fred Darby. Tickets ranged from one shilling to 2/6 which included three hours of entertainment. Fire destroyed both the auditorium and stage on the 23rd December, 1898 and the theatre wasn't opened again until May 1899.

There were twice nightly vaudeville shows by 1902 and artists who appeared during the early 1900s included Neil Kenyon billed as a 'Scotch' comedian, Robert Williams a sword swinger and Miss Gertie Gitana who sang songs including 'Nellie Dean.'

In 1909, Harry Houdini played at the theatre for a week during August and drew a huge crowd. In 1931, Charlie Chaplin, who was in Plymouth as a guest of Nancy Astor, appeared on stage on the 16th November.

The theatre stayed open during the blitz of 1941 to keep people's spirits up. Acts that appeared that year included Billy Cotton and his band, Tommy Handley, Arthur Lucan (Old Mother Riley), Henry Hall and his Orchestra as well as many less known acts. At Christmas of that year, the show was Robinson Crusoe which starred George Hirstie.

The theatre closed in 1949 for redecorating and reopened with the Billy Cotton Bandshow. The theatre closed again in 1954 due to the lack of touring shows. It was offered to the Plymouth City Council in 1956 but they refused to buy it and it closed for five months before reopening in October 1956. It closed suddenly on the 7th February, 1959 during the pantomime, 'Little Miss Muffet' because of lack of interest.

New management took over the theatre in 1961 and it became Palace Theatre (Bingo) Ltd.

The theatre reopened in 1962 with the pantomime, 'Sinbad the Sailor.'

In 1965, Arthur Fox, a businessman from Manchester, paid £50,000 for the theatre with the intention of hosting Star Bingo, wrestling (which was very popular at the time) and striptease.

In 1975, it was bought by EMI and opened on the 19th April, 1977 with a performance of 'The Magic Flute.' The theatre struggled and closed on the 27th May, 1980 when it ceased trading and its contents were put up for sale. It reopened on the 16th May 1981 for a review with Danny La Rue but finally closed in 1983 when it became the Academy Disco.

Its fortunes didn't improve and today it remains closed and its shabby appearance hides its varied history. It's amazing to think of the great acts that once appeared at the Palace and also to think of the many people in Plymouth that have been entertained by them.

The theatre is said to be haunted, a rumour started in the early 1960s.

An early poster advertising the New Palace of Theatre Varieties.
Shows were twice nightly and admission was one penny.

Management and staff at the New Palace Theatre.

The theatre's grand interior.

The fashionable Hoyles.

Thomas Hoyle was the proprietor of the New Palace Theatre and was described as being very sharply dressed and wore a black cape with a scarlet lining over his dress suit. Mr Hoyle can also be seen in the earlier photo of management and staff at the theatre. The woman, pictured, appears in both photos and is assumed to be Mrs Hoyle.

A theatre poster advertising Laurel and Hardy's appearance at the Palace Theatre.

Laurel and Hardy appeared at the Palace Theatre on 17th of May, 1954. Stan and Ollie were touring the country appearing in a show called, 'Birds of a Feather'. The shows in Plymouth were to have been their last shows of the tour. Playing on the same bill, at the time, were Harry Worth and 'Wonder Horse Tony'. Unfortunately, Oliver Hardy had a severe bout of the flu and also had a mild heart attack and the show was cancelled. Ollie spent the rest of his stay in Plymouth recovering at the Grand Hotel on the Hoe.

Laurel and Hardy had visited Britain once before in 1932 when they were mobbed wherever they went. When they returned in 1954 they were handicapped by age and illness but still managed to give an exhausting thirteen shows a week.

After they had to pull out from the show, Stan Laurel wrote a letter to the manager of the Palace Theatre, William Willis, apologising. It read:

'My Dear Mr Willis,

Please pardon delay in acknowledgement of your kind letter of the 22nd.inst. which was deeply appreciated. Many many thanks.

Mr Hardy is feeling better but, of course, is still very weak. However, we are sailing for the States on June 2nd, so I think the voyage and rest will do him a lot of good.

We too were very much disappointed, not being able to fulfil our engagement with you - unfortunate for all concerned, could have been a profitable and happy week. Anyway, we hope to have the opportunity and pleasure of meeting and playing for you again in the near future.

Mrs Laurel and Mr and Mrs Hardy join in kindest regards and every good wish always, and remember us kindly to Mr Heath, the staff and regular patrons.

Very Sincerely:
Stan Laurel.'

Benny Baron with Laurel and Hardy.

Plymouth's Barry Ewart has a connection with both the comedians as his grandfather, Benny Baron, taught Stan many of his routines. Although Barry never knew his grandfather, his mother used to tell him stories of when Benny toured the music halls with his partner, Jack Graham. Barry's uncle, Billy Baron, remembers, 'Stan adopted exactly the facial expressions my father used in his act. He was the one who got everything wrong and used to 'cry' when his partner knocked off his straw boater.'

Barry continues, 'My grandfather first worked with a young Stanley Jefferson (later Stan Laurel) in the early 1900's (before America beckoned). The first documented production I can find is a juvenile pantomine company run by H.B.Levy and J.E. Cardwell. The production was 'The Sleeping Beauty'. My grandfather Benny was older than Stan. Master Stanley Jefferson played Ebeneezer (Golliwog2) and my grandfather played Major Flashlight. Amongst others in the cast were Jack Graham (later to become my grandfather's stage partner in the double act, 'Graham and Baron'). Jack played Colonel Dreadnought. I have in my possession a letter from Stan to my grandfather (at a time when Stan was famous as one half of Laurel and Hardy) and a picture of Stan, Ollie and Benny when they toured during the 1950s. My late mother always used to refer to Stan as uncle Stan and she told me many stories. Apparently, Stan learnt the deadpan face , and the 'cry' from Benny. In the movie, 'The Flying Deuces', Babe sings shine on Harvest Moon. Stan does a soft shoe shuffle routine and this dance routine was taught to Stan step for step by Benny. My elder brother used to do part of this (my grandfather died before I was born). Apparently, Stan wanted Benny to go to America where, he explained to Benny, it was money for old rope (he was still not famous then) but my grandmother was having none of it saying it was bad enough touring round Northern England and Scotland (mostly) with their by now growing family including my mum (Irene Baron). After a long stint in variety as a double act with Jack Graham my grandfather finally retired from the stage to run a pub in Sunderland called, 'The Boars Head Hotel'. Stan always kept in touch with my grandfather.'

Barry adds, 'My grandfather lived in Sunderland and my mother (Irene Baron) came from Sunderland to Plymouth in the early fifties to marry a matelot (my dad). I might add that my mother, when she was young, sang on stage with none other than Judy Garland, allbeit in the chorus line, and most of my uncles played in the orchestra pit of the Sunderland Empire , and toured most of the theatres in Northern England.'

After their British tour, and after their visit to Plymouth where Ollie was taken ill, Laurel and Hardy travelled back to America on the 3rd June 1954 on the Danish ship, 'Manchuria'.

This photo shows a recovered Ollie on the left with Stan on the right. They're dining at the Captain's table.

Unfortunately, Ollie died three years later on the 7th August 1957. He was 65 years old.

Stan wrote about their journey back home in a letter;

'We sailed from Hull, England on June 3rd on a Danish Cargo ship. The voyage took 23 days, stopped in at St. Thomas (the Virgin Islands), Curaco Christobal and through the Panama Canal. It was very interesting, especially the Canal. The accommodations were very nice - good food and calm sea all the way, I really prefer travelling this way as you don't have to dress up for meals etc. as you do on the big passenger ships. There were only 10 passengers on this trip (12 is the limit they carry) so its practically like being on a private yacht.'

Stan died on the 23rd February 1965 at his home in Santa Monica. He was 74.

Benny Hill appeared at the Palace Theatre on Monday 17th March 1955. Benny was billed as the 'BBC's latest star comedian.' He was born Alfred Hawthorne Hill in Southampton on the 21st January 1924. Before becoming a comedian, his jobs had included being a milkman, a bridge operator, a driver and a drummer. He became an assistant stage manager and took to the stage inspired by the stars of the old music hall. He changed his name to Benny after the American comedian, Jack Benny. He started slowly touring working men's clubs, small theatres and night clubs. After the war, he worked as a radio performer. His first tv role was in 1949 in a programme called, 'Hi there!'. His career took off in 1955 when the BBC gave him his own show, 'The Benny Hill Show.' The show ran until 1968. During that time, Benny also did work for ATV. In 1969, the Benny Hill Show moved to Thames Television until 1989 when, due much to political correctness, the show was cancelled. Benny had been a huge star and had a number one hit, 'Ernie' in 1971. When the show was cancelled, Benny was forgotten by the tv channels and his health deteriorated. He needed a triple heart bypass which he declined. He died on 19th April 1992 at his home in Teddington. He was 68.

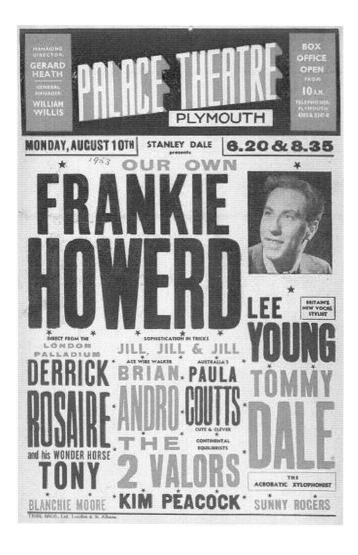

A theatre poster announcing the appearance of Frankie Howerd at the Palace.

Many of the acts that appeared with Frankie Howerd in the show are now long forgotten, although 'Wonder Horse Tony' appears on the Laurel and Hardy poster. The show took place on Monday, 10th August 1953.

Two later photos of the Palace Theatre which show the theatre as a Bingo Hall. Palace Bingo appeared in 1961. The Theatre is already showing signs of neglect in the first picture although it is not as bad as it is today.

Eight
Durnford Street

In 1773, the Edgcumbes leased out the land which was later to become Durnford Street and Emma Place. Durnford Street was named after Joan Durnford, the 15th century heiress, who by marrying into the Edgcumbe family, brought the ownership of Stonehouse and Maker into the hands of the Edgcumbe family. Emma Place was named after Lady Emma Edgcumbe and Caroline Place was named after her sister, Lady Caroline Edgcumbe. The grand houses built in the area were inhabited by the rich and successful.

At the far end of Durnford Street is the Anglican Church of St Paul. It was designed by John Foulston and was opened in 1831. When the Church of St George was destroyed in the Second World War, the two parishes were combined.

Branching off further along on the right is Admirals Hard. Regular ferries leave from the jetty and take passengers over to Cremyll on the Mount Edgcumbe Estate.

DURNFORD STREET AND R. M. BARRACKS, STONEHOUSE.

A view down Durnford Street showing Stonehouse Barracks on the left. If you were to stand in the same spot today, most of what can be seen in the older photo still remains. However, the area is a lot more busier with traffic today.

Sir Arthur Conan Doyle assisted at a medical practice at Durnford Street and Sherlock Holmes was said to be based on his colleague, Dr Budd. Conan Doyle achieved the titles of Bachelor of Medicine and Master of Surgery in 1881 and had studied with George Turnavine Budd at Edinburgh. When Budd opened a practice in Durnford Street in 1882, he asked Conan Doyle to join him. The partnership didn't last long. Although Budd and Conan Doyle were friends, Conan Doyle found his partner over prescribed drugs for his patients, for which he charged them, and was unorthodox in the extreme. He wrote and told his mother, Mary, about Budd's ways. She had never been an admirer of his. After two months, the partnership was dissolved because Budd said that it was short of both finances and patients. Conan Doyle discovered later that Budd had found one of his letters to his mother and the real reason for the break up of the partnership was that he had been upset by what he had read.

Conan Doyle left and set up a practice in Southsea with just £10 to his name. At first, it wasn't very successful and, while he was waiting for patients, he wrote his first story featuring Sherlock Holmes, 'A Study in Scarlet.'

Conan Doyle died on the 7th July 1930 aged 71. Today, passages from his works featuring Sherlock Holmes can be found on brass plaques set into the pavement at Durnford Street.

Number 1 Durnford Street where Sir Arthur Conan Doyle practiced.

The rear of Durnford Street.

Vice-Admiral Sir Thomas Masterman Hardy once lived at 156 Durnford Street. Although he rose through the ranks to become a Vice-Admiral, his Naval career is remembered by just three words, 'Kiss me, Hardy'. When Vice-Admiral Horatio Nelson was fatally wounded aboard HMS Victory in 1805, he was taken below deck where he was later visited by Hardy. Nelson's words to him were, 'Take care of poor Lady Hamilton', before he uttered the immortal words, 'Kiss me, Hardy'. It has been suggested that what Nelson actually said was, 'Kismet, Hardy' meaning that this was his fate. However, that was not the case as many officers present, including his surgeon, William Beatty, who wrote down his words, bore witness to the actual event. When Nelson uttered the words, 'Kiss me, Hardy', Hardy knelt beside him and kissed him on the cheek. Many people think that these were his last words, but his final words were uttered just before he died three hours after he had been shot. These words were, 'God and my country'.

Nine
Stonehouse Barracks

Work commenced on Stonehouse Barracks in 1781 on land purchased from Lord Mount Batten. The design followed a common theme used in other parts of Britain and comprised of three accommodation blocks which enclosed the parade ground. On its forth side was a guardroom. The north block was for junior officers, the south block was for senior officers and the lower ranks and NCOs were housed in the East block. Occupation of the barracks began in 1783.

In 1903, a nearby building, 'the Longroom', which had previously been used for balls and other entertainment, fell into disrepair so negotiations began to purchase the land so that an extension to the barracks could be built. Military forces were being increased due to the fear of invasion by French forces under the command of Napoleon Bonaparte. Lord Mount Edgcumbe sold the site for £4,450 and work began in 1805 to build a wooden barracks and the original Longroom later became the Officers mess.

When the Crimean War broke out in the 1850s, accommodation at the East block was extended to provide 28 extra rooms, with space for 30 men in each. The work was completed in 1859.

In 1861, the north block was demolished and rebuilt and in 1862, the Racquet Club became the Globe Theatre.

An early photo of the barracks.

In 1867, the west block was finished which included the entrance now seen at Durnford Street. The west block provided accommodation for six senior officers and housed the offices for the Plymouth Division.
In 1871, a Divisional School was added which fronted onto Caroline Place.

These two photos show troops within the barracks. The top photo shows a wooden fire cart complete with hose. A small dog (probably their mascot) stands on top.

An impressive parade within the barracks.

The 2nd battalion of the Devonshire regiment, 1912.

Shown here are the soldiers of No.4 Section, 'F' Company, stationed at Stonehouse Barracks. The photographer is Easden of Plymouth.

Trooping the Colour at the barracks in 1932.

After the bombing of the city in March, 1941, King George VI and Queen Elizabeth visited Plymouth including Stonehouse. Here, the King can be seen inspecting the troops on the parade ground of the barracks.

Ten

The Royal Naval Hospital

With no permanent Naval hospital in Plymouth Dock and only a hospital ship, the Canterbury, the decision was made to build a permanent hospital in the area.

In 1756, a piece of land called No Place Field, on the southern side of Stonehouse Creek, was purchased by the Commissioners for the Sick and Wounded Seamen. The land was bought from Henry Tolcher but proved too small and was left undeveloped for 68 years.

In 1758, the Commissioners purchased five fields from the Mount Edgcumbe family at a cost of £2,239, 17 shillings and 16 pence. The fields lay between No Place Field and the creek. Worked commenced on the building of the hospital and by 1760, a small part of it was opened for patients. Previously, sick and wounded seamen had been cared for in a building in George Street in Stonehouse.

In 1762, the patients that had been receiving treatment on the Canterbury were moved to the new buildings within the hospital.

The piece of land at No Place Field which remained unused became the Royal Naval Hospital Burial Ground in 1824.

In 1830, a native from Terra Del Fuego was buried within the grounds of the hospital. He was one of four men brought back to England on HMS Beagle by Captain Robert Fitzroy in the same year. The 24 year old native, who Fitzroy had named, 'Boat Memory', had earlier been transferred to the hospital and he, and the other three natives, later unfortunately all died of smallpox.

Seamen who died from their wounds at the hospital were buried on the grounds and the last burial took place in 1897. The were no burials within the grounds after that time apart from one exception. In 1912, the wife of Staff Captain Moore was allowed to be buried with her late husband.

During the Second World War, twenty four bombs landed on the hospital. One block was totally destroyed and two others were severely damaged. When the burial ground was acquired by the St Dunstan's Abbey School in 1956, the area was used as a playing field and the headstones were placed around the boundary wall.

In later years, the hospital continued to treat Naval personnel as well as civilian patients.

The hospital was closed in 1995 and today houses 'Millfields' - an upmarket gated community with its own security guards.

Two photos showing the Royal Naval Hospital. The first shows the
spacious grounds of the Naval Hospital with neatly lawned gardens.
Three women appear to be having a picnic on the right of the
picture.
The second photo shows the accident ward which had been made
to look as homely as possible complete with flowers and a dining
table.

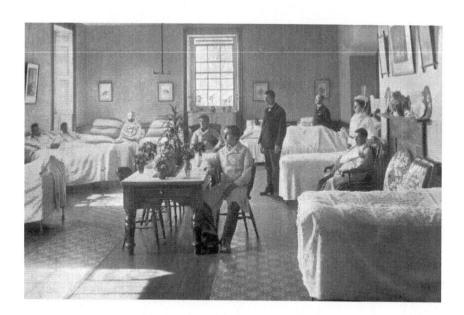

A patient arriving at the hospital by boat. The landing jetty wasn't used much after the First World War.

The Naval Officers based at the hospital.

The head of the hospital was Sir Henry F Norbury KCB who was the Inspector General of Hospitals and Fleets.

Norbury was born on 12th September 1839 and was educated at Oundle School and at St Bartholomew's Hospital. He entered the Navy as a surgeon in 1860 and in 1898, he succeeded Sir James Dick as Director General of the Medical Department of the Navy. He retired in September 1904 and died on 10th December, 1925.

The nurses stationed at the hospital. They appear to be sat on a large suitcase. One is holding a small flag.

The sick berth attendants.

Some of the patients at the hospital, many were elderly.

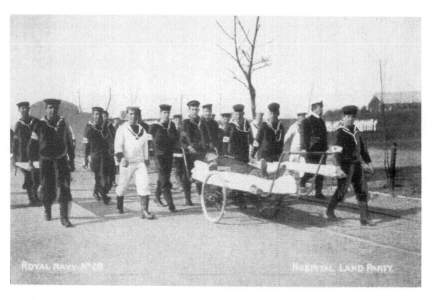

An injured seaman is taken to the hospital on a stretcher trolley.

Eleven
Devil's Point

Devil's Point was originally called Cremhill (Crimble) Point and was so named because of the ancient ferry that carried passengers between there and Cremell (later Cremyll) across the Hamoaze. Originally, the ferry landed at Barn Pool but in 1730 it was moved to its present landing place at Cremyll because of the upset it caused to the Edgcumbes. The landing place at Cremhill Point was later moved to Mutton Cove in 1750 and sometime after moved to its present location at Admiral's Hard. A Huguenot refugee called Duval took up residence at Devil's Point and some say that this is why the name was changed from Cremhill Point. The name Cremhill Point appears on maps until 1846.

RN sailors at Western King Point, Stonehouse.

There are three Tudor fortifications to be found in the area of Devil's Point. All date from the time of Henry VIII. They were put in place to defend the mouth of the river. One can be found across the water at Barn Pool and, at one time, regular crossings were made there from Western Kings. The two fortifications on the Plymouth side are to be found at Firestone Bay and further around at Eastern Kings close to the entrance at Millbay. The fortification at Firestone Bay, built in the 1500s, was converted into a restaurant in 1983. Its previous uses had been as a police house, a coastguard station, a store for the Ministry of Defence and a public convenience.

The Chapel of St Lawrence once stood at Devil's Point but it was removed in the 18th century to make way for the Victualling Yard that would later be built there. The Folly at Mount Edgcumbe contains parts of St Lawrence together with parts of the nearby St George Chapel.

Devil's Point still has the remains of defensive posts, pill-boxes and anti-aircraft gun emplacements from the Second World War.

Devil's Point or Western King Point showing some of the older buildings that have since disappeared.

Charles Darwin.

At Devil's Point, there is a plaque commemorating the sailing from Barn Pool, at Mount Edgcumbe, of HMS Beagle.

Charles Darwin's journey is mentioned in the Quarterly Review of 1840:

'On the 27th November, 1831, the well-manned, well-appointed and well-provided Beagle sailed from Barn Pool, and having circumnavigated the globe, and accomplished all the objects the expedition had in view, as far was practical, she anchored at Falmouth on the 2nd October, 1836, after and absence of four years and nine months.'

Darwin had lived in Plymouth for two months before his famous voyage around the world in HMS Beagle. The ship was captained by Robert Fitzroy. Darwin, who was then just 22 years old, joined the crew as a naturalist. He had a wealthy family who paid the £30 fare needed to travel on the Beagle.

When he returned to England, he married Emma Wedgwood, the daughter of the potter, Josiah Wedgwood.

He carried on his research and in 1859, his book, 'The Origin of the Species by Natural Selection' was published.

Darwin died in 1882 at his home in Orpington, Kent. He is buried at Westminster Abbey.

Twelve
The Royal William Victualling Yard

Work commenced on the Royal William Victualling Yard in 1826. It was designed by Sir John Rennie to be used by the Admiralty as a victualling base for the Royal Navy.

The whole site coved an area of 16 acres, including 6 acres of land that were recovered from the sea.

The cost of the yard was approximately £2 million and it was completed in 1835. By then, the Duke of Clarence had succeeded to the throne and had become King William IV. By order of the Admiralty in 1833, it was named the Royal William Victualling Yard after William IV who was the last Lord High Admiral.

A statue of King William IV stands over the grand entrance of the yard in Cremyll Street. The statue stands 13 feet 9 inches and is surrounded by sculptures of the trades that were once incorporated within the yard including bakers, coopers and butchers.

The gateway to the Royal William Victualling Yard.

Royal William Yard in the late 1800s.

Looking from Mount Wise towards Royal William Yard.

Two older photos showing Royal William Yard. In the first photo, the buildings all look much the same as they do today although nowadays there are many luxury boats and yachts moored nearby. The second photo shows an old paddle steamer.

Thirteen

Millbay Docks

The docks were designed by Isambard Kingdom Brunel and Millbay was linked to the railway in 1849. The docks soon became a port of call for the Irish Steamship Company and Brunel's services were further engaged for the construction of an extra pier which could hold 4,000 tons of coal. The docks became one of the main coaling stations in the English Channel.

Many marine and engineering businesses set up nearby to the docks to service the many vessels belonging to the Royal Mail Steamship Company, the War Department, HM Customs and many others. Passenger numbers grew and many luxury liners called at the docks. As well as regular passengers, there were many celebrities that disembarked at Millbay. These included John F Kennedy, John Wayne, General Allenby, Charlie Chaplin, Maurice Chevalier, Winston Churchill, Clemenceau, Bebe Daniels, Marlene Dietrich, Walt Disney, Douglas Fairbanks, Helen Keller, Pierre Laval, Vivian Leigh, Lloyd George, Ben Lyon, Anna Pavlova, General Pershing, Mary Pickford, Cecil Rhodes, Bernard Shaw, General Smuts and HG Wells.

Offloading goods at the docks.

The Millbay Drill Hall adjacent to the Docks.

The Mileage Yard at Millbay in the late 1800s.

An aerial view of Isambard Kingdom Brunel's Millbay Docks.

The SS Royalist docks at Millbay carrying a cargo of grain.

The Discovery at Millbay Docks prior to Captain Scott's Polar Expedition.

The Discovery was specially built in 1901 for Scott's expedition and was a wooden sailing ship which included auxiliary engines. It was modelled on a whaling ship, also called the Discovery, which had been on a previous expedition to the Arctic in the 1870s.
The ship was built in Britain and designed to withstand being stuck in ice. The propeller and rudder could be lifted to avoid them being damaged by the severe cold temperatures of the water. When she left the shipyard at Dundee in 1901, she was the first ship to be built in Britain specifically for a scientific expedition and cost a total of £50,000.
The total budget for the expedition was £92,000.

Robert Falcon Scott was born in Plymouth on the 6th June 1868. He was a British Naval Officer and explorer who led two expeditions to Antarctica. The first, the Discovery Expedition lasted three years and began in 1901. His second expedition, the Terra Nova Expedition, which commenced in 1910, is more well known and was the expedition where, unfortunately, he lost his life. Scott led a team of five men in a race to reach the South Pole. When he arrived on the 17th January 1912, he discovered that he had been beaten to the position by the Norwegian, Roald Amundsen and his team. Scott and his team, which included Edward Wilson, H R Bowers, Lawrence Oates and Edgar Evans, made their way back but died of a combination of the cold, hunger and exhaustion.

Millbay Docks in the late 1800s with many wooden hull vessels.

Scott was born at Outlands House, his family home, in the Parish of Stoke Damerel. He was a distant descendant of Sir Walter Scott and he was the father of the naturalist, Peter Scott. Outlands has now gone and St Bartholomew's Church stands in its place. Within the church is a piece of wood bearing Scott's name. In 1908, Scott had carved his name on a tree at Outlands, from where the wood was taken.

Scott was 43 when he died and his body, and that of his comrades, remain at the camp where he was found. A wooden cross was erected on top of a high cairn of snow which covered the camp.

A memorial stands to Scott at Mount Wise in Devonport.

Scott's memorial at Mount Wise.

The stewardesses from the Titanic at Millbay Docks.

On 28th April 1912, the Titanic survivors were brought back to Millbay Docks, fourteen days after the ship had sank. At 8am, the SS Lapland moored at Cawsand Bay with the 167 members of the Titanic who hadn't been detained in New York for the American inquiry. Three tenders left Millbay Docks to collect the passengers and the 1,927 sacks of mail that had been scheduled to be carried by the Titanic. The third tender, the Sir Richard Grenville, carrying the survivors, killed time in the Sound while the dock labourers and porters were paid off and escorted out of the dock gates at West Hoe. After midday, the tender was given the all clear and the survivors were allowed to disembark in an air of secrecy. They were then put on a special train from Millbay Docks to Southampton where they arrived at 10.10pm that night.

Fourteen

King Street

King Street ran from Cambridge Street to Stoke Road and Manor Street. The above photo dates from the early 1960s and shows the arch, which was just after 144 King Street which can just be seen on the left of the photo. Number 144 housed Cole's grocery shop.

Perhaps one of the most remembered shops in King Street was Ivor Dewdney's pasty shop which was at number 2 and opened in the 1930s. The photo shows interesting adverts for both Ovaltine and the Co-op.

In the early part of the last century, hawkers and entertainers gathered underneath the arch. One was a Mr Pratt who, with his monkey, Bruce, entertained passersby with his organ grinder. Bruce wore a red hat and jacket and was well-known to the people living in the area. Mr Pratt, his wife and his monkey all lived in one tiny room in the street. Small audiences would gather to watch Bruce and would feed him chipped potatoes which were sold in the evening by Italians living in the area. By day, they would sell ice cream around the town from their small handcarts.

Another well-known figure was a blind Cornish miner who sold boot and shoe laces which were draped from his left arm while, with his right hand, he would hold out a tin cup to collect money.

Many beer houses sprung up in the area during the 1850s including the Thistle Rose and Shamrock, the Hen and Chicken and the Botanic

Garden which was near Flora Street Nursery. In the shadow of the railway embankment stood the Robert Burns, the Broad Gauge and the Tandem Inn.

As a barrel organ played, bruised fruit was sold at knock down prices and women gathered to attend late night auctions selling cheap cuts of meat. Chestnut sellers would also ply their trade from a warm fire and a man on stilts would tap on windows to announce forthcoming events such as the fair or the circus. Rabbit formed a staple part of people's diet and a rabbit catcher with four or five rabbits hanging from his arm would sell and skin the creatures on the spot.

It all seems a world away from the King Street of today. Torn apart in the Second World war, the area has seen a lot of changes and rebuilding. When the arch was pulled down in the 1970s, a major part of the street disappeared and the hawkers and entertainers from nearly 100 years previous, were soon forgotten.

A different view of King Street showing an ice cream seller on the right complete with his hand cart. The several cars in this picture would probably date it to about 1960.

Fifteen
Millbridge

Sir Piers Edgcumbe was responsible for building Millbridge, and the corn mills to be found there, in 1525.

In about 1884, it was decided to fill in the upper part of Stonehouse Creek known as the Deadlake. It formed part of the mill pond for Stonehouse Mill. The Deadlake had become a health hazard and a petition was organised which was then put to the three local authorities of Plymouth, Devonport and Stonehouse who agreed to purchase it from the Earl of Mount Edgcumbe in 1890. In 1895, 400 tons of rubble was used to fill the Deadlake. Some of it came from the old tram depot at Compton although much of the rubble came from the quarries at Cattedown and Oreston. The area was reopened as Victoria Park in 1898.

A busy scene at Millbridge. At one time, a toll had to be paid to cross the bridge which once crossed a tidal estuary. Today, the area on the left, that was once taken up by the creek, is now Victoria Park.

The Deadlake was also the scene of suicides and one was reported in the Western Morning News:

The Western Morning News, 15th June, 1883.
Sad suicide at Stoke.

A widow, named Kate Parkyn Andrews, aged 52, who lived at 62, Hotham-place, Stoke, committed suicide early on Wednesday morning by drowning herself in the Dead Lake. Deceased's husband died about twelve years ago, and she has recently lived at Hotham-place with her son Henry and her other children. She was in very comfortable circumstances, as her four sons, who held very good positions, assisted her. She had, however, unfortunately given way to drink during the past few weeks, and had at times left the house at night (on one occasion staying out all night), besides doing other unusual acts in order to frighten her children. There was, undoubtedly, an inherent tendency to insanity in her disposition. Her sister is at present confined in a lunatic asylum, and her brother disappeared mysteriously some years ago. For sometime past her family had considered the advisability of confining her also, but yielding to her entreaties had, somewhat foolishly, allowed her to remain at home. On Tuesday night, the deceased, who was not quite sober, went to bed about eleven o'clock. She slept with her daughter Kate, to whom she remarked that she wished to go out, but she was persuaded to go to bed. About four o'clock the daughter awoke and found that her mother was not in bed. The window, which was 12 or 14 feet from the ground, was open, and the curtain was flying out. After a little time she called her brother, Henry, but they concluded that this was only one of the deceased's freaks, and made no stir about the matter, although the other windows, as well as the doors of the house, were all secured. Before going away in the morning, about 6 o'clock, Henry made an unsuccessful search for his mother. Nothing was heard of her until the afternoon, when, on the tide receding in Mill Lake, her body was found about twenty yards from the shore by a mason's labourer named James Smith. She was only partially dressed. Smith and a fellow labourer at once took the body to Hotham-place, and handed it over to her friends. A coroner's jury assembled last evening at the No Place Inn, and returned a verdict of 'Suicide whilst temporarily insane'.

An old photo showing the barrier crossing the toll road.

Victorian children play beside the dam and mill near to the toll road.

The tale of the Stoke gibbet is a dark and macabre one. It is a true story that tells of the murder of a dockyard clerk on the night of July 21st, 1787. Philip Smith was brutally bludgeoned to death near to Stoke Church. His murderer, a John Richards, together with an accomplice, William Smith, were both soon apprehended. Richards was a dock worker who had earlier been suspected of killing a Fore Street sentinel. At first, there were no clues to who had committed the crime but Richards soon boasted of the crime and was, shortly afterwards, arrested. However, there was little evidence against him and he was soon released. A hat found beside the body was identified as belonging to Richards' accomplice, William Smith. Hearing of this, Smith fled to Dartmouth but was soon caught and admitted to his role in the murder and implicated Richards. Both men were tried for murder at Heavitree. They were found guilty, condemned to death and executed in 1788.

The judge in the case, Judge Buller, declared that their bodies wouldn't be given to surgeons for dissection, which was usually the case, but were to be 'suspended between Heaven and Earth as they were fit for neither.' The corpses were brought from Exeter to Stoke and displayed near the scene of the crime. This gruesome practice was common at the time.

The bodies were hoisted in wire cages and chains on a gibbet erected on the muddy Deadlake beach just below Stoke Church. Smith's body stayed there for seven years before the gibbet collapsed and Richards' body stayed there slightly longer.

People avoided the spot and it was said to be 'the terror of some and the disgust of many'. Nettleton's 'Stranger's Guide to Plymouth' says that the gibbet stood in place upwards of 38 years near the Mill-bridge until it was blown down in the gale of 1827.

In 1788, a bestseller called, 'The Genuine Account of the Trial of Richards and Smith' sold 25,000 copies. Some were sold around the base of the gibbet.

Long after the gibbet disappeared, people shunned the area after dark which, during the 1830s, left the area quiet enough for grave robbers to carry out their grim practices in the secluded Stoke churchyard.

Toll lifting day at Millbridge.

Tolls were lifted on 1st April, 1924.

Molesworth Road from the crossroads at Millbridge.

The shop fronts and houses are still there today.

Sixteen
Wyndham Square

Wyndham Square was developed in the 1830s as part of John Foulston's major development of the area between Plymouth and Stonehouse. Originally, the square surrounded a non-conformist chapel which was replaced by St Peter's Church which was built between 1880 and 1882. Terraces were built to the north and south of the square. Densham Terrace was completed by 1848 followed by the development of the east side of Cecil Street.

Arundel Crescent was developed by 1865, and much of the area between Arundel Crescent, Wyndham Street East and Archer Terrace was completed by 1867. The area around Wolsdon Street and Wyndham Street West was developed by 1881.

St Boniface's College.

Founded in 1900, St Boniface's was run by the Presentation Brothers from Ireland.

The building is still there on the approach towards the front of the church.

The spire of St Peter's Church was completed in 1906.

The church was badly damaged in the Second World War during the Blitz of 1941 but was later rebuilt by Frederick Etchells and was re-consecrated in 1956.

Seventeen

Victoria Park

Between 1870 and 1899, the area known as 'Deadlake' or 'Stoke Damerel Flete' was converted into Victoria Park. A local man, Bill Parsons, who was a sewerman by trade, dug several pits eighteen feet apart and ladders were placed down manholes to stop men from being swept away.

The Deadlake had been considered a great health hazard so the land was purchased by the Earl of Mount Edgcumbe in 1890 and opened as a park the following year. During 1895, 400 tons of rubble were deposited in the lake and this process continued until 1906.

The park was officially opened in 1902 by the Mayor of Plymouth, Mr JA Bellamy. Six thousand people turned up to witness the event and thirty policemen were in attendance. The music was supplied by the Royal Marines Band and the festivities concluded with a cricket match.

Children playing at Victoria Park in the early 1900s.

Eighteen

The People

Union Street Infants, c.1900.

In the front row of the second photo, in similar dresses, can be seen four sisters of the Legg family. The Union Street School was situated at Summerland Place and opened on 27 July 1883. The headmistress of the infants school was a Miss Mary Yeo. Union Street Infants School was bombed and destroyed during the Second World War.

Cora Pearl

Cora Pearl was said to have been born in Caroline Place, Stonehouse on 23rd February, 1842. However, it is believed that she forged her birth certificate and was actually born in London in 1835. Her family moved to Plymouth in 1837.

She was born Emma Elizabeth Crouch and would become a famous courtesan of the French demimonde in the 19th century.

Pearl had inherited her musical talent from her father, Frederick Nicholas Crouch, a composer and cellist. In 1867, she appeared in the role of Cupid in a production of Jacques Offenbach's, 'Orpheus in the Underworld'.

While working in London, she became involved in prostitution and had dalliances with several wealthy men. She became the mistress of Robert

Bignell who owned the Argyll Rooms in Regent Street. Together they travelled to Paris where she first adopted the name, Cora Pearl. She fell in love with Paris and refused to return to London with Bignell.

Pearl began a theatrical career in Paris but was more known for her sexual appeal than her acting talents. Her theatrical reputation grew and she was soon linked with several wealthy men including the Duke of Rivoli. While she was with him, she developed a serious gambling habit and Rivoli, tired of bailing her out, eventually ended their affair.

She soon attracted other rich and powerful men who became her benefactors.

A skilled craftsman could earn between two or four francs a day, whereas Cora earned 5,000 a night. She was famous for dancing nude on a carpet of orchids and bathing before guests in a silver tub of champagne.

The Duke of Grammont-Caderousse said at the time, 'If the Freres Provencaux served an omelette with diamonds in it, Cora would be there every night.'

Her lovers included Prince Willem of Orange, Prince Achille Murat and the Duke of Morny. Morny was Napoleon III's half-brother. Being financially sound, she rented Chateau de Beausejour in 1864, which lay on the banks of the Loiret outside Orleans.

When Morny died in 1865, Cora became the mistress of Prince Napoleon who was the cousin of Emperor Napoleon III. He purchased two homes in Paris for her and also supported her financially until 1874.

Although her activities made her very wealthy, her downfall resulted from her compulsive gambling and ultimately, her age. One story though seems to have led more to her downfall than others. She was the mistress of the wealthy Alexandre Duval who lavished her with gifts and money. When she chose to end the affair, Duval was so distraught that he shot himself on her doorstep. Rather than call for assistance or help him, she went back inside and went to bed. Duval survived but stories of the incident spread quickly and brought her theatrical career to a halt. She fled back to London but her popularity had waned and she eventually returned to Paris. With no benefactor to support her, she had to sell her possessions to support herself. In 1886, she became ill with intestinal cancer and had to move to a shabby boarding house where she died in poverty and forgotten by most.

The staff of W H Parkhouse in Battery Street in 1895.

**Members of the St John Ambulance Association, Stonehouse
Section, in Rendle Street, complete with bicycles.**

The St John Ambulance Association together with other members of the community. They have their own mascot - a young boy also dressed in the uniform of the St John Ambulance division.

Stonehouse residents holding a Garden Fete in the Winter Villa in 1912.

Putty Philpotts can be seen in this photo dressed as Carnival King leading the Plymouth, Stonehouse and Devonport Carnival in 1926. Although he was a Devonport man, Putty is remembered for being the landlord of the No Place Inn at Eldad Hill.

Well-known across the city, he was described as a giant of a man. This wasn't just because of his weight but also because of his jolly and generous personality. The Carnival, which raised money for the Royal Albert Hospital, lasted all week and included parades, fancy dress and much entertainment. Thousands of people attended the Carnival over the seven days.

Putty had a varied career. At twenty stones, he had once been the heaviest man in the Navy. When he left the services, he became the landlord of the Brunswick Hotel in High Street, Stonehouse. He would entertain customers by playing the banjo and singing songs beside the log fire in the public bar. Stars from shows at the Palace Theatre would attend and join in the fun. Putty liked to rewrite the words of popular songs and 'South of the Border' became 'South of the Border Down Stonehouse Bridge Way'.

Unfortunately, The Brunswick Hotel was destroyed by a land mine during the Second World War. Putty took over a pub in Devonport but, coincidently, this was bombed on the very first night he was there.

Putty was also known for appearing in local concerts where he would entertain people with his songs, one of which was 'Figgy Pudding'. Putty died at the No Place Inn and his pallbearers, so the story is told, drank to his memory before the funeral so that 'they could be fortified before carrying out their bulky task!'

This photo shows Putty Philpotts outside the Royal Albert Hospital in 1926. Also in the picture are members of the Carnival procession including the Carnival Queen who is believed to be Edith Mayne. Nurses from the hospital also appear in the photo.

A later photo showing Carnival Week in Rendle Street in 1933. Before the War, these events were very popular all over the city and many areas held their own Carnival with thousands of people attending during the week.

Richard Greene was born in Stonehouse on the 25th August, 1918. He appeared in 'The Adventures of Robin Hood' for 143 episodes between 1955 and 1960.

His aunt was Evie Greene, an actress in musical theatre, and his parents were both actors with the Repertory Theatre in Plymouth. He was educated in Kensington and left school when he was 18. His stage career began when he played a spear carrier in a version of Julius Caesar in 1933. In 1936, he joined the Jevan Brandon Repertory Company and appeared in Terence Rattigan's 'French Without Tears' where he came to the attention of Alexander Korda and Darryl F Zanuck. When he was 20, he joined 20th Century Fox and became a huge success after appearing in John Ford's movie, 'Four Men and a Prayer.' He received so much fan mail that he rivalled Tyrone Power and Robert Taylor. Greene continued to make movies until he enlisted in the 27th Lancers during the Second World War.

Greene appeared in propaganda films during the war and also toured entertaining the troops. However, the war ruined Greene's rising film career although he is well remembered for 'Forever Amber' which was made in 1947. Afterwards, he found himself cast in mainly swashbuckling roles. With little film work and his divorce from Patricia Medina, Greene was almost forgotten when he was approached by Yeoman Films who offered him the lead role in 'The Adventures of Robin Hood.' By taking the role it solved his financial problems and also made him a huge star. Richard Greene died at his home in Norfolk on the 1st June, 1985.

Valetort Primary School football team 1951.

The Valletort Primary School football team.

This photo taken in 1952 includes Mr Stevens, Mr Hannaford, Peter Edmunds, Ed Roberts, Tommy Turner, Pete Dinham, George Swabey, Pete Thurston and Brian Woodman. The school is situated in High Street.

Members of Woodrow Metals football team, Blight and White 'Steel United.'

Featured in this photo are Gordon Stevens, Dave Parsons, George Wright, Bob Harper, Frank Lampley, Percy Putt, Bobby Putt, Gordon Stewart, Brian Stewart and Frankie Jago.

Bill Cole in his grocer's shop at 144 King Street.

The original business sold rabbits, which in those days, were staple food for most families. They were sold from a store beside the shop.

John Cole, who lived at 144 King Street, as a choir boy at a local church.

The choir master, a Mr Hurden, was also a music teacher at Stuart Road Secondary Modern School. Boys were paid on attendance for choir practice and Sunday service.

Nineteen
The Second World War

The blitz during the Second World War completely changed the face of much of Stonehouse. The Town Hall and areas near to Emma Place were completely destroyed. Damage was also done to the Stonehouse Bridge and parts of Union Street.

The bridge was first opened in 1773 and in 1828 the bridge was raised so that Hackney carriages could provide a public service from Plymouth to Devonport. Here, part of it is severely damaged by a nearby bomb blast.

Edgcumbe Street and Stonehouse Bridge.

A policeman surveying the damage in Union Street.

The badly damaged shop on the right is 'Weaver to Wearer', the 30 shillings tailors. They also had a shop where the old Criterion Cinema once stood in Cornwall Street. On 27th January 1941, there was a huge explosion at Coxside when an attempt to reconnect the gas supply was unsuccessful. Three men were killed and five were injured and ominous bulges were noticed in Union Street caused by broken gas mains.

Jay's Furnishing Stores, The Octagon, Union Street.

On 21st March 1941, large parts of Union Street were bombed and the entire Octagon was ringed with fire as Jay's and Service and Co's premises burnt. Further back, in the Crescent, the hotels, Westminster and Hackers were completely destroyed.

Union Street.

Much of Union Street lies shattered or destroyed in this picture although the road has been cleared of debris so that traffic can still flow through. On the right, is a temporary gas supply pipe running along the kerbside. The railway ran right over an arch at the top of Union Street and this and the nearby Millbay Station became a target for bombing.

The Millbay Laundry, Stonehouse.

The laundry had an air raid shelter underneath in a reinforced basement. Millbay was a target not just because of the train station but also because of the nearby docks. It was the Germans aim to disrupt life as much as possible by disrupting supplies and travel.

Bombing of Millbay Station.

Naval personnel help clear away the rubble.

Looking down Frankfort Street towards King Street.

The Odeon Cinema can be seen in the background. The poster in the background reads, 'Go To It!'

The captured German Submarine U-1023.

As the American presence within Plymouth grew, it became obvious that Plymouth was to be a major leaving point for the invasion of Europe. Their activity, although top secret, could be seen at hards, slipways, wharfs and basins especially in the Saltash Passage and Cattewater areas.

This photo taken in East Street shows two white-capped US Naval policemen who were quick to sort out any trouble that arose. A US sailor stands in the doorway. Their headquarters shown here was at St George's Hall which was also used by the Royal Navy shore patrols after the war until the 1950s.

Here are some of the US Navy's Shore Patrol complete with their jeeps, again pictured at St George's Hall. Their job was to police the thousands of US personnel on duty in the Plymouth area.

Victory Day Party 1945.

This photo shows a party held to celebrate Victory Day. It included people from Admiralty Street, St Paul's Street, Durnford Street and the surrounding areas. The Victory Queen was Eileen Edmunds.

Handbells rung in the remains of St George's, Stonehouse. St George's Church was located in Chapel Street in East Stonehouse. After the church was damaged by bombing, later services were held at St Paul's Church in Morice Square, Devonport. In 1957, the council bought the church for £1,400 and the stonework was used to build the Lady Chapel at St Gabriel's Church in Mutley.

Twenty

Stonehouse Today

Durnford Street.

Admiral's Hard showing the ferry leaving for Cremyll.

St Paul's Church, Durnford Street.

King Street looking towards Frankfort Gate.

Royal William Yard.

Stonehouse Barracks, Durnford Street.

Devil's Point.

St Peter's Church, Wyndham Square.

Books by the same author:
Images of England : Plymouth (Tempus 2003).
Plymouth at War (Tempus 2006).
Sampans, Banyans and Rambutans : A Childhood in Singapore and Malaya (Driftwood Coast Publishing 2006).
Saltash Passage (Driftwood Coast Publishing 2007).
St Budeaux (Driftwood Coast Publishing 2007).
Plymouth Hoe (Driftwood Coast Publishing 2008).
Mount Edgcumbe (Driftwood Coast Publishing 2009).
Memories of Singapore and Malaya (Driftwood Coast Publishing 2007).
More Memories of Singapore and Malaya (Driftwood Coast Publishing 2009).
Saltash (Driftwood Coast Publishing 2008).
Memories of St Budeaux (Driftwood Coast Publishing 2009).
Plymouth : Tales from the Past (Driftwood Coast Publishing 2010).
Monsoon Memories (Driftwood Coast Publishing 2010).
Plymouth Through Time (Amberley Publishing 2010).
Saltash Through Time (Amberley Publishing 2010).
Rame Peninsula Through Time (Amberley Publishing 2010).
Sampans, Banyans and Rambutans (Amberley Publishing 2011).
Plymouth from Old Photographs (Amberley Publishing 2011).
Plymouth at War Through Time (Amberley Publishing 2011).
The River Tamar Through Time (Amberley Publishing 2011).
A Year on the Tamar (Amberley Publishing 2011).
A 1970s Childhood (The History Press 2011).
Houdini : The British Tours (Driftwood Coast Publishing 2011).